D0686810

Bluthenthal, Todd,
Making maps /
2018.
33305241478985
sa   06/06/18

MAKING MAPS

By Todd Bluthenthal

Gareth Stevens
PUBLISHING

Please visit our website, www.garethstevens.com. For a free color catalog of all our high-quality books, call toll free 1-800-542-2595 or fax 1-877-542-2596.

Cataloging-in-Publication Data

Names: Bluthenthal, Todd.
Title: Making maps / Todd Bluthenthal.
Description: New York : Gareth Stevens Publishing, 2017. | Series: Where on Earth? mapping parts of the world | Includes index.
Identifiers: ISBN 9781482464252 (pbk.) | ISBN 9781482464276 (library bound) | ISBN 9781482464269 (6 pack)
Subjects: LCSH: Map drawing—Juvenile literature. | Maps—Juvenile literature.
Classification: LCC GA130.B58 2017 | DDC 526—dc23

Published in 2018 by
Gareth Stevens Publishing
111 East 14th Street, Suite 349
New York, NY 10003

Copyright © 2018 Gareth Stevens Publishing

Designer: Samantha DeMartin
Editor: Joan Stoltman

Photo credits: series art CHAPLIA YAROSLAV/Shutterstock.com; cover, p. 1 (protractor) Gearstd/Shutterstock.com; cover, p. 1 (compass tool) Olga Popova/ Shutterstock.com; cover, p. 1 (navigation compass) canbedone/Shutterstock.com; p. 5 Rob Marmion/Shutterstock.com; p. 7 Peter Hermes Furian/Shutterstock.com; p. 9 Icons vector/Shutterstock.com; p. 11 (map) olenadesign/Shutterstock.com; p. 11 (compass rose) Olegro/Shutterstock.com; p. 13 Aleksandr Markin/ Shutterstock.com; p. 15 Mastak A/Shutterstock.com; p. 17 StockLite/Shutterstock.com; p. 19 Daxiao Productions/Shutterstock.com; p. 21 (pencil, eraser) MichaelJayBerlin/ Shutterstock.com; p. 21 (markers) Vichy Deal/Shutterstock.com; p. 21 (compass) Rost9/Shutterstock.com; p. 21 (paper) Zhukov/Shutterstock.com.

All rights reserved. No part of this book may be reproduced in any form without permission in writing from the publisher, except by a reviewer.

Printed in the United States of America

CPSIA compliance information: Batch #CS17GS: For further information contact Gareth Stevens, New York, New York at 1-800-542-2595.

CONTENTS

What's a Map? 4

Scale 6

Direction 10

Perspective 12

The Key 14

Map Your Street! 16

Glossary 22

For More Information 23

Index 24

Boldface words appear in the glossary.

What's a Map?

Maps show where places are and how close they are to each other. Maps can also show **information** about a place! Cartographers, or mapmakers, use **perspective** when they make maps. They include a key and directions to help read the map!

Scale

When you're making a map, the paper will likely be much smaller than what you're mapping. Using a scale fixes this problem for cartographers like you. A scale tells what a measurement on the map means in **distance** on Earth. Each map has its own scale.

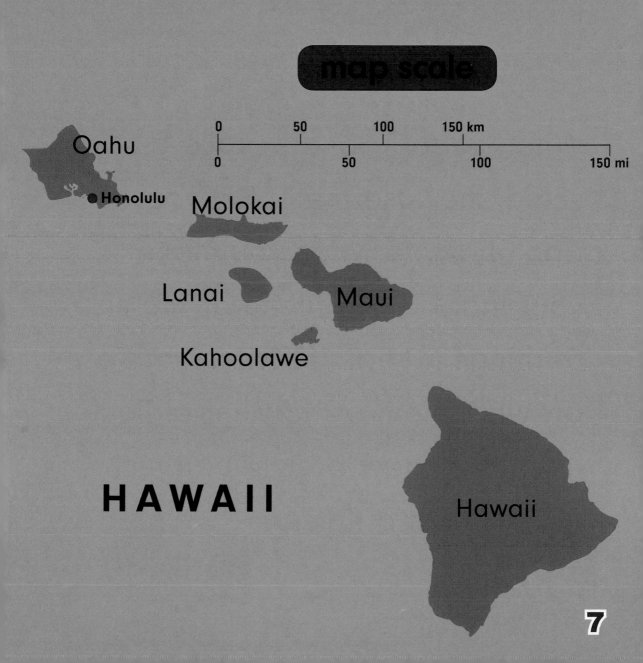

map scale

0   50   100   150 km

0   50   100   150 mi

Oahu

● Honolulu

Molokai

Lanai

Maui

Kahoolawe

HAWAII

Hawaii

7

When cartographers make a scale, they use math. But you don't have to when you make your map! Just remember the size of things in real life when you're drawing them on your map. For example, draw a building much bigger than a flower.

9

Direction

Using a map would be hard without knowing which way is north. A compass rose is a **symbol** cartographers use to help people read their maps. Use a compass rose to tell readers which way is north on your maps.

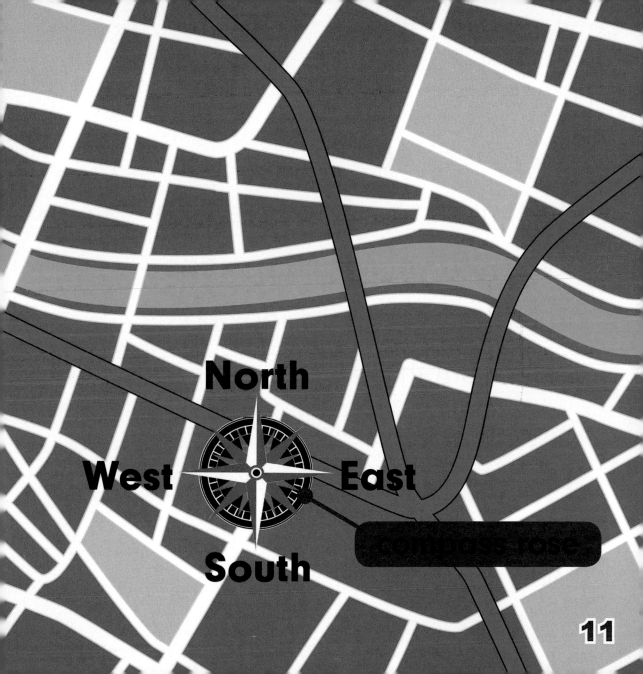

North

West

East

South

compass rose

11

Perspective

Most maps show a place from above. When making a map, pretend that you are looking down from the sky like a bird. This perspective is called "bird's-eye view"! What do you see? How far apart are the things you see?

The Key

After you've decided what will be on your map, **assign** each thing a color, symbol, or line. You can show water as blue and houses as orange squares. Roads can be black lines. Make a key to show what the symbols, lines, and colors mean.

MAP KEY

	roads
🔵	**land**
🔺	**schools**
	houses
	city hall
	**water**

Map Your Street!

First, take a good look at where things are on your street. Go out your front door. Are you standing on the lawn? What's to your left and right? Think about how far your home is from the buildings next to it. Where is the street?

17

Next, take a walk down your street to gather information. Have an adult walk with you and help you write down what you see. Point out parks, roads, friends' houses, trees, street signs, and even dogs! Make sure you take a **compass** and write down which way is north!

Back inside, draw the shape of your street down the middle of a piece of paper. Draw each part of your street in the order they are on the street, but from a bird's-eye view! Color it, and then make your key and compass rose.

WHAT YOU'LL NEED TO MAKE A MAP

GLOSSARY

assign: to match one thing with another thing

compass: a tool for finding directions

distance: the amount of space between two places

information: facts

perspective: a way of showing how close or far places are that matches the facts in the real world

symbol: a picture or shape that stands for something else

FOR MORE INFORMATION

BOOKS

Boswell, Kelly. *Maps, Maps, Maps!* North Mankato, MN: Capstone Press, 2014.

Sweeney, Joan. *Me on the Map.* St. Louis, MO: Turtleback Books, 2015.

Waldron, Melanie. *Mapping Communities.* Chicago, IL: Capstone Raintree, 2013.

WEBSITES

Are You Map-Savvy?
socialstudiesforkids.com/articles/geography/mapsavvy1.htm
Read about all the different types of maps!

Cat in the Hat Mapping Tool
pbskids.org/catinthehat/games/mappingtool.html
Make a colorful online map of anything you want!

Map Maker 2.0
mrnussbaum.com/mapbuilder2/
Make your own United States or world map.

Publisher's note to educators and parents: Our editors have carefully reviewed these websites to ensure that they are suitable for students. Many websites change frequently, however, and we cannot guarantee that a site's future contents will continue to meet our high standards of quality and educational value. Be advised that students should be closely supervised whenever they access the Internet.

INDEX

bird's-eye view 12, 20

cartographers 4, 6, 8, 10

color 14

compass 18

compass rose 10, 20

distance 6

information 4, 18

key 4, 14, 20

line 14

measurement 6

north 10, 18

perspective 4, 12

scale 4, 6, 8

symbol 10, 14